THE SCIENCE OF
ELECTRICITY & MAGNETISM

PROJECTS AND EXPERIMENTS
WITH ELECTRICITY AND MAGNETS

© 2005 Heinemann Library
a division of Reed Elsevier Inc.
Chicago, Illinois

Customer Service 888-454-2279
Visit our website at www.heinemannlibrary.com

Designer: David West
Editor: Gail Bushnell
Picture Research: Gail Bushnell

09 08 07 06 05
10 9 8 7 6 5 4 3 2 1

Library of Congress Cataloging-in-Publication Data

Parker, Steve.
   The science of electricity & magnetism : projects and experiments with electricity and magnets / Steve Parker.
      p. cm. -- (Tabletop scientist)
   Includes index.
   ISBN 1-4034-7283-1 (library binding-hardcover) -- ISBN 1-4034-7290-4 (pbk.)
   1. Electricity--Experiments--Juvenile literature. 2. Magnetism--Experiments--Juvenile literature. I. Title: Science of electricity and magnetism. II. Title.
   QC527.2.P377 2005
   537--dc22

                                        2005006945

Acknowledgments
The author and publisher are grateful to the following for permission to reproduce copyright material:
Pages 4t, 10, 12 – Corbis Images. 8t (Roger-Viollet); 18–19 (Sipa Press); 22–23 – Rex Features Ltd.

With special thanks to the models: Meshach Burton, Sam Heming De-Allie, Annabel Garnham, Andrew Gregson, Hannah Holmes, Molly Rose Ibbett, Margaux Monfared, Max Monfared, Charlotte Moore, Beth Shon, Meg Shon, William Slater, Danielle Smale and Pippa Stannard.

Printed and bound in China

THE SCIENCE OF
ELECTRICITY
& MAGNETISM

PROJECTS AND EXPERIMENTS
WITH ELECTRICITY AND MAGNETS

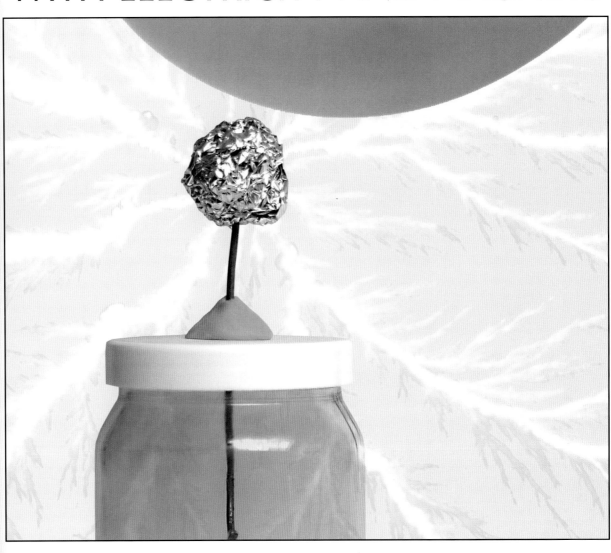

STEVE PARKER

Heinemann Library
Chicago, Illinois

CONTENTS

From microcircuits far too small to see...

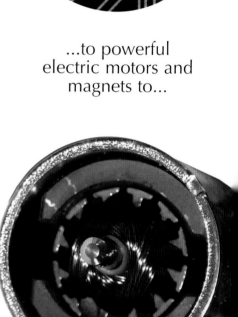

...to powerful electric motors and magnets to...

...coating things with shiny hard metal, the twin technologies of electricity and magnetism affect our daily life in countless ways.

INTRODUCTION

The world gets busier and more electromagnetic. Electricity lets us do many things from making a phone call to cleaning our clothes. Wherever there is electricity, there is also magnetism. Electricity is our favorite form of energy. We can make it, we can transfer it from place to place easily, we can get it to carry information, and we can convert it back to other forms of energy. All of these processes rely on our knowledge of the sciences of electricity and magnetism.

HOW IT WORKS

These panels explain the scientific ideas in each project and the processes that make it work.

Prepare each project carefully and follow the instructions. Remember: real scientists always put safety first.

WARNING
- Adults should oversee all experiments.
- All wires should be insulated.
- Do not ever touch a conductor when it is connected to an electrical current.
- Never connect the two terminals of a battery, or series of batteries, directly together.
- Do not experiment with a car battery.
- Never experiment with electrical sockets.

Where you see these symbols:

 Ask an adult to help you.

 Project should be done outdoors.

 Sharp tools may be needed.

 Prepare work surface for a messy project.

1.5v battery   9v batteries

Batteries have a positive (+) terminal and a negative (−) terminal. You will need 1.5v and 9v batteries. Either type of 9v battery will do.

TRY IT AND SEE

These panels show more ideas for you to try so that you can experiment and find out more about electricity and magnetism.

STATIC ELECTRICITY

Static electrical charge on a rubbed balloon pulls or attracts very light items that do not carry electric charge very well. They include pieces of tissue paper, feathers, dust, and human hair.

Electricity is made by tiny particles called electrons. These are even smaller than the atoms which make up all substances and materials. In fact, electrons are inside atoms, whirling around and around. Electrons have an electric charge. When they leave their atoms and go toward another they cause electricity.

In each atom, electrons go around the central part, called the nucleus.

PROJECT: MAKE A CAPACITOR (CHARGE-HOLDER)

CHARGE-HOLDER

WARNING!
Do not charge the carrier more than about ten times. Otherwise you may get a small shock!

WHAT YOU NEED

- polystyrene plate and cup
- camera film canister
- nail
- aluminum foil
- wire
- foil tray

1	2	3	4
POUR WATER INTO A PLASTIC FILM CANISTER OR SIMILAR SMALL PLASTIC CONTAINER. FILL IT ABOUT TWO-THIRDS OF THE WAY UP AND FIRMLY CLIP ON THE LID.	VERY CAREFULLY AND ON A FIRM BASE, TAP A NAIL WITH A HAMMER SO IT GOES THROUGH THE LID. MAKE SURE THE NAIL GOES DOWN FAR ENOUGH TO ENTER THE WATER.	FOLD SOME ALUMINUM FOIL INTO A STRIP AND SMOOTH IT AROUND THE LOWER HALF OF THE CANISTER.	GLUE THE RIM OF A POLYSTYRENE CUP TO A FOIL TRAY. THIS IS THE CHARGE CARRIER TO CONVEY ELECTRICAL CHARGE TO THE CANISTER, WHICH IS THE CAPACITOR.

STATIC TO MOVING

Rubbing the plate on the carpet makes atoms lose some of their electrons. Electrons have a negative charge, so the remaining atoms are positive. This positive charge transfers to the foil tray and then to the nail and water. The positive charges in the canister attract electrons as negative charges in the aluminum foil. When the wire links the two, electrons travel along it from the foil into the nail to even out the charges and restore balance.

JUMPING ELECTRONS MAKE A SPARK

POSITIVE CHARGES

NEGATIVE CHARGES

MAGIC PULL

Rub materials like plastic, nylon, wool, and acrylic. See how the charges that build up on them attract small pieces of tissue paper.

TRY CHARGING A NYLON COMB WHEN IT IS DRY, THEN WET. DOES THE WATER LET THE CHARGE LEAK AWAY?

5

6

7

RUB A POLYSTYRENE PLATE BRISKLY FOR A FEW SECONDS ON A CARPET OR CLOTH MADE FROM WOOL OR NYLON. THE DRIER THE CONDITIONS, THE BETTER THIS PROJECT WILL WORK.

HOLD THE CHARGE-CARRIER BY THE CUP. TOUCH ITS ALUMINUM TRAY ONTO THE POLYSTYRENE PLATE. THIS TRANSFERS THE ELECTRIC CHARGE FROM THE PLATE ONTO THE TRAY.

TOUCH THE FOIL TRAY TO THE NAIL SO THE CHARGE CAN ENTER THE CAPACITOR. REPEAT THE CHARGING PROCESS (5 AND 6) 10 TIMES TO INCREASE THE CHARGE IN THE CAPACITOR.

ZZZZAP
ATTACH A WIRE TO THE BASE. MAKE SURE YOU DO NOT TOUCH THE NAIL WHILE YOU DO THIS. HOLD THE WIRE AND GRADUALLY MOVE ITS END TO THE NAIL. EVENTUALLY THERE WILL BE A CRACK AS THE ELECTRONS JUMP. IF YOU DO THIS IN A DARK ROOM YOU SHOULD SEE A SPARK AS WELL.

HOW MUCH CHARGE?

In 1752, Benjamin Franklin flew a kite in a thunderstorm to show that lightning happens because of electric charge. The charge traveled down the damp string and caused a spark when it jumped from a key. Franklin was amazingly lucky, as he could have been killed.

Until two hundred years ago, static charge was the only kind of electricity that scientists could use. It was stored in capacitors (then called Leyden jars), and it made cracks and sparks as it jumped from one substance to another. During experiments it was important to measure the amount of charge. In fact it still is, since many electrical devices today use modern types of capacitors.

PROJECT: MAKE A CHARGE MEASURER (ELECTROSCOPE)

CHARGE MEASURER

WHAT YOU NEED

- glass jar with plastic lid
- thick, stiff wire (e.g. coat hanger wire)
- aluminum foil
- modeling clay
- balloon
- hammer
- nail
- wire cutters

1 TAKE THE LID OFF THE GLASS JAR. MAKE A SMALL HOLE IN THE CENTER OF THE LID WITH A HAMMER AND NAIL, JUST WIDE ENOUGH FOR THE THICK METAL WIRE TO PASS THROUGH.

2 CUT OFF A SHORT LENGTH OF THE THICK, STIFF WIRE. BEND THE END AT A RIGHT ANGLE TO FORM AN L-SHAPE. PUSH THE WIRE THROUGH THE LID HOLE AND FIX IT FIRMLY WITH MODELING CLAY.

3 BEND A STRIP OF ALUMINUM FOIL OVER THE LOWER END OF THE WIRE, LIKE A THIN UPSIDE-DOWN V. ROLL MORE FOIL INTO A TIGHT BALL. PUSH THIS ONTO THE UPPER END OF THE WIRE.

PUSH-PULL

Different charges attract one another. The same charges repel one another. Positive charges on the balloon attract negative ones up the wire to the ball, leaving positive charges on the foil strip. The positive charges on the strip's sides repel each other and make the sides push apart.

POSITIVE CHARGES ON BALLOON

NEGATIVE CHARGES ON BALL

POSITIVE CHARGES PUSH APART

PUSHED APART
BLOW UP A BALLOON AND RUB IT ON WOOL OR NYLON MATERIAL SO ELECTRIC CHARGE OR STATIC COLLECTS ON ITS SURFACE. BRING THE BALLOON NEAR THE FOIL BALL, BUT WITHOUT TOUCHING IT. WATCH THE FOIL STRIP—ITS SIDES MOVE FARTHER APART! MOVE THE BALLOON AWAY AND THE STRIPS MOVE CLOSER TOGETHER AGAIN.

MEASURE

The greater the charge, the farther the strip's sides push apart. Charge used to be measured this way.

TRY USING THE CHARGED CAPACITOR FROM PAGE 6.

4

PUT THE LID BACK ONTO THE JAR. THE FOIL STRIP INSIDE SHOULD HANG DOWN FREELY WITH ONLY A VERY NARROW SPACE BETWEEN THE TWO SIDES OF ITS V SHAPE.

CIRCUITS AND SWITCHES

In static electricity, electrons stay close to home. In current electricity, like that created by a battery, the electrons flow steadily along a pathway or circuit made of a suitable substance. These substances are called electrical conductors and are mainly metals.

In a complex circuit the electricity can flow along hundreds of different pathways.

PROJECT: MAKE A CIRCUIT WITH TWO-WAY SWITCHES

CIRCUIT WITH TWO-WAY SWITCHES

1 DRAW PICTURES ON PAPER OF THE UPSTAIRS, STAIRS, AND DOWNSTAIRS OF A HOUSE.

2 GLUE THE PICTURES ONTO THE CARDBOARD, WITH SPACE AROUND THEM FOR THE CONDUCTORS.

3 CUT LONG STRIPS OF ALUMINUM FOIL AS CONDUCTORS AND GLUE THEM TO THE BOARD AS SHOWN.

WHAT YOU NEED

- cardboard
- paper
- two 1.5-volt batteries
- 3-volt lightbulb in holder
- foil
- wire
- pins

4

5

CUT A CARDBOARD CIRCLE WITH A SIDETAB AND GLUE THE SAME SHAPE OF FOIL TO ONE SIDE, AS A SWITCH. MAKE ANOTHER. ATTACH THEM FOIL-DOWN WITH PINS.

GLUE THE LIGHTBULB-HOLDER TO THE CARDBOARD. THE BATTERIES MUST TOUCH + TO –-.
RUN A WIRE FROM THE LOWER BATTERY TO THE LOWER FOIL STRIP, ONE FROM THE UPPER BATTERY TO THE LIGHTBULB, AND ONE FROM THE LIGHTBULB TO THE UPPER STRIP.

6

UPSTAIRS, DOWNSTAIRS

A SWITCH BREAKS THE CIRCUIT OF CONDUCTORS BY PUTTING AN AIR SPACE INTO IT, AND AIR IS A VERY POOR CONDUCTOR. A ONE-WAY SWITCH IS EITHER ON, ALLOWING ELECTRICITY TO FLOW, OR OFF, STOPPING THE FLOW. IN THIS TWO-SWITCH CIRCUIT, EACH SWITCH CONTROLS THE FLOW.

THE LIGHT IS ON (BELOW LEFT) AS ELECTRICITY FLOWS THROUGH THE LEFT-HAND FOIL STRIP. IF YOU FLICK THE DOWNSTAIRS SWITCH...

...THE CIRCUIT IS BROKEN BECAUSE THERE IS NO CONNECTION BETWEEN THE TWO FOIL STRIPS. SO THE LIGHT GOES OUT (ABOVE). THEN LATER...

...WHEN YOU ARE UPSTAIRS, YOU MIGHT WANT TO TURN THE LIGHT ON. FLICKING THE UPSTAIRS SWITCH MAKES A COMPLETE CIRCUIT AGAIN BECAUSE ELECTRICITY CAN NOW FLOW THROUGH THE RIGHT-HAND FOIL STRIP (ABOVE). SO THE LIGHTBULB GLOWS AGAIN. THIS WORKS TIME, AFTER TIME, AFTER TIME...

FLOWING CHARGES

If an electron is given enough "push," it leaves its atom and looks for another atom that lacks an electron. A battery provides enough "push" for all the electrons to do this along a metal wire.

As a result, billions of electrons all do the same, hopping from one atom to the next in the same direction along the wire. This flow of charges or electrons is called an electric current.

ATOM   **ELECTRON**

NUCLEUS

FLOW OR NO FLOW?

In high-power electricity cables, the insulators look like stacked disks made of special ceramic material.

Electricity does not flow out of plugs, sockets, and devices such as televisions, because air does not allow it. Substances that carry electricity are conductors. Those that do not are called insulators. Electrical wires are made to be good conductors. Air is a good insulator. What about other everyday substances and materials?

Most metals are good conductors. One of the best is copper, above being wound as wire on to large reels. Millions of miles are used for wiring in buildings and electrical machines.

PROJECT: BUILD A CONDUCTION TESTER

CONDUCTION TESTER

WHAT YOU NEED

- electrical wires
- thumb tacks
- 3-volt lightbulb
- 1.5-volt battery
- foam board
- tape

TAPE A BATTERY AND A LIGHTBULB IN ITS HOLDER TO THE FOAM BOARD BASE. CONNECT ONE LIGHTBULB CONTACT TO ONE END OF THE BATTERY WITH WIRE. ATTACH LONGER WIRES TO THE OTHER END OF THE BATTERY AND THE OTHER LIGHTBULB CONTACT AND PIN AS SHOWN.

COLLECT A WIDE RANGE OF EVERYDAY OBJECTS MADE OF DIFFERENT MATERIALS TO TEST. WILL THEY CONDUCT OR NOT?

BRIDGING THE GAP

Electricity only flows when it has a complete pathway or circuit of conductors. If a conductor bridges the gap between the wire ends, electrons move and make the lightbulb light. Insulating materials prevent this.

PRESS ON WIRE END FIRMLY

TEST OBJECT

LIGHTBULB IN HOLDER

BATTERY

SEMI-FLOW?

Put the "lead" of a pencil, which is really the substance graphite, across the gap. The lightbulb may glow slightly. Graphite is a weak conductor and lets through some electricity but not all.

TRY PENCILS OF DIFFERENT LENGTHS. IS THERE A BRIGHTER GLOW WITH A SHORTER PENCIL? WHAT ABOUT THE WOOD OF THE PENCIL?

GLOW OR NO GLOW?

TO TEST A MATERIAL, PLACE THE OBJECT IN THE SPACE BETWEEN THE ENDS OF THE LONGER WIRES. HOLDING THE WIRES BY THEIR PLASTIC COVERINGS, PRESS THEIR BARE METAL ENDS ONTO THE OBJECT TO MAKE A GOOD CONNECTION. IF THE LIGHTBULB GLOWS, THE MATERIAL IS A CONDUCTOR. IF NOT, IT'S AN INSULATOR.

Resist the Flow

Good insulators hold back or resist the flow of electricity. They have very high resistance. Good conductors have very low resistance and let electricity through. In some circuits and machines, there's a need to change the amount of resistance.

A dimmer switch alters the glow of a lightbulb from full brightness to almost none.

Project: Make a dimmer switch

1. Wind a piece of plastic-coated wire around a large cardboard tube in neat coils, side by side. Push the bare ends into holes at the tube's ends.

2. Wrap sandpaper around a wooden block. Use it to rub the plastic coating from the wire in a long strip to leave the wire's bare metal exposed.

3. Fix the battery, the lightbulb in its holder, and three lengths of wire onto a foam board base as shown for the conduction tester on the last page. Join one of the long wires to the wire at one end of the tube.

MORE = LESS

Even copper wire puts up a small resistance to electricity. The longer the wire, the greater this resistance, so less electricity flows around the circuit. As you move the "wiper" along the coil from left to right, electricity must flow through more turns. More wire means less electricity and therefore a dimmer lightbulb.

ELECTRICITY FLOWS THROUGH ONLY A SHORT PART OF THE COIL

ELECTRICITY FLOWS THROUGH A LONGER PART OF THE COIL

BRIGHTER AND DIMMER
THE FREE END OF THE LONG WIRE IS THE "WIPER." HOLD IT BY THE PLASTIC COVERING AND TOUCH IT TO THE EXPOSED WIRE ON THE COIL. SLIDE IT BACK AND FORTH ALONG THE COIL, PRESSING TO KEEP A GOOD CONTACT. DOES THE LIGHTBULB CHANGE BRIGHTNESS?

JUST AS DIM?

Obtain a bare length of pencil "lead" or graphite (see previous page) as used in mechanical pencils. Put this in place of the wire coil. Does the dimmer still work?

TRY MAKING THE COIL WITH THE TURNS FARTHER APART. THE LIGHTBULB MAY GLOW BRIGHTER, BUT IS THE WIPER EASY TO USE?

ADD UP OR SHARE

A simple circuit has a battery and lightbulb connected by wires. Increasing the number of parts, or components, in a circuit also increases the number of different ways they can be connected. One way is components in series so electricity flows through them one after the other. Another is in parallel (side by side) so electricity passes through them at the same time.

Flashlight batteries are in series, one behind the other. If they are both 1.5 volts, together they produce 3 volts.

In a battery charger, the batteries are in parallel. Each one receives the full amount of charging electricity.

PROJECT: TEST CIRCUIT DESIGNS

CIRCUIT DESIGN TESTER

WHAT YOU NEED

- cardboard
- glue
- aluminum foil
- electrical wire
- two 1.5-volt batteries
- two 3-volt lightbulbs
- tape

MAKE A CIRCUIT BOARD FROM FOIL STRIPS GLUED TO A BASE (ABOVE). PREPARE LENGTHS OF ELECTRICAL WIRE TO LINK THE BATTERIES, LIGHTBULBS, AND FOIL STRIPS IN VARIOUS WAYS.

BATTERIES IN SERIES

PLACE TWO BATTERIES INTO THE UPPER SPACE, + OF ONE TOUCHING – OF THE OTHER. TAPE A WIRE FROM EACH REMAINING BATTERY CONTACT TO THE FOIL. CONNECT THE BULB INTO THE LOWER SPACE. IS ITS GLOW BRIGHT?

TWO 1.5-VOLT BATTERIES IN SERIES PRODUCE A TOTAL OF 1.5 + 1.5 = 3 VOLTS

FOIL STRIPS CONNECT TWO BATTERIES TO LIGHTBULB IN HOLDER

3-VOLT LIGHTBULB IS DESIGNED TO SHINE BRIGHTLY WHEN 3 VOLTS PASS THROUGH IT

CIRCUITS AND SUMS

For two batteries put together in series, their "pushing strength" in volts is twice as much. For batteries put together in parallel, the volts stay the same. However, the amount of electricity, which is the current measured in amps, is twice as much. If lightbulbs are put together in series, the resistance of each one, measured in ohms, adds up.

If the batteries are put together in parallel, their resistances are "shared" and so they are less. Scientists use a rule called Ohm's Law to determine the volts, amps, and ohms in a circuit, depending on the way components are put together.

MORE DESIGNS

Try similar experiments to those on the left, but use only one battery. This time connect the lightbulbs in series and then parallel, as shown below. How do you think the lightbulbs will light up?

BATTERIES IN PARALLEL

USE THE SAME CIRCUIT BOARD, CONNECT ONE BATTERY INTO THE UPPER SPACE AND ONE INTO THE MIDDLE SPACE. LEAVE THE LIGHTBULB IN THE LOWER SPACE. THE LIGHTBULB NOW GLOWS LESS BRIGHTLY BUT IF LEFT ON, IT WOULD SHINE FOR LONGER THAN WITH BATTERIES IN SERIES.

TWO LIGHTBULBS IN SERIES INCREASE RESISTANCE IN CIRCUIT AND SHINE DIMLY

SINGLE BATTERY PRODUCES 1.5 VOLTS

TWO 1.5-VOLT BATTERIES IN PARALLEL PRODUCE A TOTAL OF 1.5 VOLTS BUT MAKE THE LIGHTBULB GLOW FOR TWICE AS LONG

3-VOLT LIGHTBULB SHINES LESS BRIGHTLY WHEN ONLY 1.5 VOLTS PASS THROUGH IT

SINGLE BATTERY PRODUCES 1.5 VOLTS

TWO LIGHTBULBS IN PARALLEL DECREASE RESISTANCE IN CIRCUIT AND SHINE BRIGHTER

MYSTERY MAGNETISM

Magnetism is a mysterious force. We cannot see it, but we can feel a magnet push or pull against other objects—especially other magnets. A magnet has "opposite" poles, north or + and south or –.

PROJECT: MAKE A MAGLEV TRAIN

WHAT YOU NEED

- **plenty of small bar magnets**
- **thick cardboard or foam board**
- **glue**
- **scissors**
- **screwdriver**

1 GATHER 12 OR MORE SMALL BAR-SHAPED MAGNETS. IT MAY BE POSSIBLE TO "BORROW" THEM TEMPORARILY FROM REFRIGERATOR MAGNETS BY PRYING THEM OUT GENTLY WITH A SCREWDRIVER.

2 GLUE THE MAGNETS TO THE TRACK—A LONG NARROW CARDBOARD STRIP. ENSURE THE SAME POLE OF EACH FACES UP (SEE PANEL OPPOSITE).

3 CUT OUT TWO MORE LONG, THIN STRIPS OF CARDBOARD. GLUE THEM TO THE EDGES OF THE TRACK TO GIVE IT SMOOTH SIDES.

4 CUT OUT A CARDBOARD STRIP THREE MAGNETS LONG AND $\frac{1}{8}$-INCH WIDER THAN THE TRACK FOR THE TRAIN. GLUE ON THE MAGNETS. BE SURE THE SAME POLES FACE DOWN AND THESE ARE THE SAME AS THE POLES FACING UP ON THE TRACK. CUT TWO CARDBOARD SIDES FOR THE TRAIN.

TRAIN MAGNETS

TRACK MAGNETS

Maglev means "magnetic levitation" (lifting). The train has no wheels. Magnetic forces make it "float."

LAW OF MAGNETISM

Like electric charges, magnetic poles show pushing or pulling forces. The basic law is that the same poles, such as north and north, or south and south, push apart. Different poles, north and south, pull together. The law says: "Like poles repel, opposite poles attract."

OPPOSITE POLES ATTRACT

LIKE POLES REPEL

5

GLUE THE SIDES ONTO THE TRAIN. MAKE SURE IT FITS OVER THE TRACK. THE SIDES KEEP IT UPRIGHT. IF THE TRAIN CLAMPS DOWN HARD ONTO THE TRACK, ONE SET OF MAGNETS IS ON THE WRONG WAY!

6

MAKE A TOP FOR THE TRAIN BY CUTTING OUT THE PAPER SHAPE SHOWN ABOVE. FOLD IT ALONG THE DOTTED LINES AND GLUE THE OVERLAPPING FLAPS.

7

THE FINISHED TRAIN LOOKS SOMETHING LIKE THIS. MAKE THREE CARDBOARD STANDS TO SUPPORT THE TRACK AT AN ANGLE.

SILENT SLIDE

PLACE THE TRAIN AT THE TOP OF THE TRACK AND LET IT GO. IT SHOULD SLIDE DOWN SMOOTHLY AND QUIETLY. THE POLES OF THE TRACK AND TRAIN MAGNETS REPEL TO MAKE THE TRAIN "HOVER."

DIFFERENT SHAPES

All magnets have a north and a south pole.

TO FIND THE POLES, HOLD A PAIR OF MAGNETS TOGETHER AND FEEL WHERE THE FORCES ARE STRONGEST.

MAGNETIC WORLD

Magnetism affects mainly iron-containing substances. The center or core of the Earth is very hot iron, which makes our whole planet into a giant magnet. This is why the names North and South Pole apply both to magnets and to the entire Earth. We use a much smaller

A compass is vital for walkers, sailors, explorers, pilots, and others on long journeys.

magnet to detect Earth's magnetic forces, using the basic law of magnetism from the previous page.

PROJECT: MAKE A COMPASS

COMPASS

DRAW A CIRCLE ½-INCH SMALLER THAN THE JAR LID AND CUT IT OUT. COLOR A PATTERN ON IT WITH A BLACK ARROW.

CUT A LARGE SQUARE OF CLEAR LAMINATING PLASTIC. SMOOTH IT OVER THE COLORED SIDE OF THE PAPER CIRCLE.

STROKE THE NEEDLE IN THE SAME DIRECTION WITH THE SAME POLE OF A MAGNET OVER 300 TIMES. IT BECOMES A MAGNET TOO.

WHAT YOU NEED

- paper
- steel sewing needle
- magnet
- plastic jar lid
- clear laminating plastic
- scissors
- colored pens or paints

TEST THE NEEDLE'S N AND S POLES (PAGE 19). TAPE IT WITH ITS N UNDER THE BLACK ARROW.

APPLY ANOTHER SQUARE OF LAMINATING PLASTIC OVER THE NEEDLE AND CIRCLE AS A SEAL.

TRIM THE PLASTIC AROUND THE CIRCLE, LEAVING ¼-INCH EXTRA AS A CLEAR EDGE ALL AROUND.

MAGNETIC FIELD

A magnet's forces are like lines between the poles, called lines of magnetic force. Earth's lines of force go from the North to South Pole. Held level, the compass needle's poles are attracted by Earth's poles and point to them. At Earth's poles the lines of force enter the ground almost at right angles, but around Earth's middle they are parallel with the ground. Put a compass on its side pointing North and South, and its needle shows this angle, called dip or inclination. The whole area of magnetism is the magnetic field.

NORTH POLE

ALL LINES OF MAGNETIC FORCE MAKE UP MAGNETIC FIELD

COMPASS ON ITS SIDE ALIGNS WITH DIP ANGLE OF LINES OF MAGNETIC FORCE

SOUTH POLE

COMPASS POINTS TOWARDS EARTH'S NORTH POLE

COMPASS FLOATS FREELY IN WATER

NORTH POLE OF MAGNETIZED NEEDLE IS UNDER BLACK ARROW

WHICH WAY IS NORTH?
PUT SOME WATER IN THE JAR TOP. PLACE YOUR COMPASS IN THE WATER AND WATCH AS IT TURNS TO FACE NORTH. IF YOU USE IT OUTSIDE, PUT THE GLASS JAR OVER THE TOP. THIS WILL STOP THE WIND FROM AFFECTING IT.

SEE IT!

You can see a magnet's lines of force by placing the magnet under thin paper. Sprinkle iron filings on the paper and tap gently. What do you see?

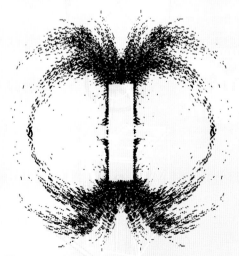

TRY THIS WITH DIFFERENT SHAPES OF MAGNETS, LIKE BUTTONS, HORSESHOES (U), AND RINGS.

ELECTRICAL MAGNETS

Electricity and magnetism are "twins." They almost always occur together, as one of the most basic or fundamental forces in the universe, electromagnetism. When electricity flows, it makes a magnetic field around itself. If the electricity stops, the field stops. Electromagnets make great use of this on/off magnetism.

PROJECT: MAKE AN ELECTROMAGNET

Electromagnets are used in scrapyards to lift many tons of weight.

ELECTROMAGNET

WARNING! Electromagnets may become hot if they are left on for too long. Do not touch the nail in case this happens.

WHAT YOU NEED

- **cardboard tube**
- **large iron nail**
- **electrical wire**
- **1.5-volt battery**
- **aluminum foil**
- **cardboard**
- **tape**
- **scissors**
- **straw**

1. TRIM THE STRAW SLIGHTLY LONGER THAN THE NAIL. INSERT THE NAIL INTO THE STRAW.

2. THREAD THE WIRE THROUGH THE STRAW, TOO. WIND IT TO MAKE A HALF-COIL WITH FREE ENDS.

3. CUT THREE CARDBOARD CIRCLES THAT JUST FIT INTO THE TUBE. MAKE HOLES IN TWO WITH A PENCIL.

4. SLIDE THE CARDBOARD CIRCLES OVER THE STRAW. TAPE ONE WIRE END TO A PIECE OF FOIL AND GLUE THIS TO THE END CARDBOARD.

5. SLIDE THE ASSEMBLY OF CARDBOARD CIRCLES, NAIL, STRAW, AND WIRE COIL INTO THE TUBE. THE COIL PART STICKS OUT OF ONE END.

6. PUT A BATTERY IN THE TUBE, ONE CONTACT TOUCHING THE FOIL. THE WIRE SHOULD RUN PAST THE BATTERY TO ITS OTHER END.

A USEFUL TOOL

PUSH THE REMAINING CARDBOARD CIRCLE INTO THE TUBE END TO PRESS THE WIRE ONTO THE BATTERY CONTACT. ELECTRICITY FLOWS AND THE NAIL BECOMES A MAGNET. TRY PICKING UP SMALL IRON OR STEEL ITEMS WITH YOUR ELECTROMAGNET, LIKE PAPER CLIPS AND SEWING PINS.

LINING UP

Iron is full of tiny areas of magnetism called domains. Normally these point in different ways and cancel each other out (1). A flow of electricity nearby makes the domains line up, so that all their north poles point the same way (2). This turns the whole iron object into an electromagnet.

1

2

SOUTH

CIRCUIT OF ELECTRICITY

NORTH

STRONGER

Test the strength of your electromagnet by seeing how many pins it can pick up. Can you think of any ways to make it stronger or weaker?

TRY MORE TURNS OF WIRE IN THE COIL AND TEST ITS STRENGTH. ALSO TRY FEWER TURNS FARTHER APART OR A STRONGER BATTERY.

ELECTRIC PULL

A car's central locks use a two-way solenoid in each door to lock or unlock.

Electromagnets can be used to make movements. A typical electromagnet has a coil of wire wrapped around an iron rod, the core, that does not move. A solenoid is an electromagnet with a core that can move. If the core is not fully inside the coil when the electricity switches on, it is pulled inside.

PROJECT: MAKE A SOLENOID LOCK

A loudspeaker moves back and forth due to magnetic forces on the coil of wire at the back.

SOLENOID LOCK

WARNING! Solenoids, being similar to electromagnets, may become hot if they are left on for too long. Do not let the electricity flow for more than a few seconds.

WHAT YOU NEED

- straw
- paper clips
- electrical wire
- 9-volt battery
- cardboard or foam board
- glue
- scissors
- pencil
- electrical tape

1

CUT OUT THREE 1-INCH SQUARES OF THICK CARDBOARD OR FOAM BOARD. MAKE A STRAW-SIZED HOLE IN THE MIDDLE OF TWO OF THEM USING A PENCIL.

2

CUT A ½-INCH LENGTH OF STRAW. GLUE IT UPRIGHT TO THE THIRD SQUARE.

3

CUT OUT A BASE ABOUT 5 INCHES SQUARE AND AN UPRIGHT STAND ABOUT 3 INCHES BY 6 INCHES. CUT A SLOT IN THE MIDDLE OF THE BASE JUST BIG ENOUGH FOR THE BOTTOM EDGE OF THE STAND. GLUE THE STAND INTO THE SLOT. GLUE THE THREE SQUARES TO THE STAND, PROJECTING FORWARD LIKE SHELVES AS SHOWN. THE DISTANCE BETWEEN THE TOP AND MIDDLE SQUARES WILL BE THE LENGTH OF THE SOLENOID.

4

TRIM A PIECE OF STRAW ½-INCH LONGER THAN THE LENGTH OF THE SOLENOID. COIL THE WIRE AROUND THE STRAW MANY TIMES, LEAVING LONG FREE ENDS. STRAIGHTEN A PAPER CLIP TO MAKE THE INNER ROD, OR CORE.

PULLED TO THE CENTER

When electricity flows along a straight wire, the magnetism around the wire is very weak. In a wire coil, the magnetism around all the turns adds together to produce a much stronger force. The magnetism in an electromagnet is exactly the same as in an ordinary or permanent magnet. It attracts nearby objects made of iron. The paper clip core is steel, which consists mainly of iron. So the core is pulled forcefully into the center of the magnetic field.

SOLENOID COIL MAKES A MAGNETIC FIELD WHEN ELECTRICITY FLOWS.

CONNECTIONS TO BATTERY

SOLENOID CORE IS PULLED INTO COIL BY MAGNETIC FORCE.

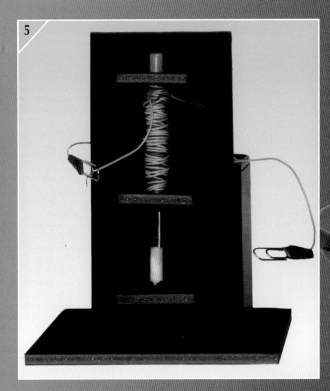

5

PUT THE STRAW INTO THE HOLES IN THE UPPER AND LOWER SQUARES. DROP THE PAPER CLIP DOWN THE STRAW TO REST IN THE LOWER STRAW. CONNECT TWO PAPER CLIPS WITH ELECTRICAL TAPE TO TWO PIECES OF WIRE THAT ARE ATTACHED TO THE BATTERY TERMINALS.

LOCK ... UNLOCK ... LOCK ...

WHEN YOU CONNECT THE PAPER CLIPS TO THE WIRES FROM THE COIL, ELECTRICITY FLOWS AND MAKES A MAGNETIC FIELD. THIS PULLS THE CORE UP INTO THE MIDDLE OF THE COIL AND "UNLOCKS" THE LOWER STRAW. WHEN THE ELECTRICITY STOPS, GRAVITY PULLS THE CORE BACK DOWN AND "LOCKS" THE STRAW AGAIN.

MOTOR POWER

Car-sized motors in electric trains move hundreds of tons of cars, passengers, and cargo.

Electricity and magnetism are combined to make a spinning motion in one of the world's most useful inventions—the electric motor. Some motors are smaller than pinheads. Others are bigger than trucks. But they all depend on split-second timing to switch on electricity and magnetism.

Most electric motors have many sets of windings to give smooth and powerful rotational motion.

PROJECT: MAKE AN ELECTRIC MOTOR

ELECTRIC MOTOR

WARNING! The wire must be thin but stiff and have a thin covering or coating of insulation. Be especially careful removing part of this coating in stage 4.

WHAT YOU NEED

- thin coated electrical wire
- 2 large paper clips
- disc magnet
- 9-volt battery
- cardboard or foam board
- glue
- dull knife

1

CUT A CARDBOARD OR BOARD BASE AND UPRIGHT STAND EACH ABOUT 8 INCHES LONG. GLUE THE STAND ONTO THE BASE.

2

STRAIGHTEN EACH LARGE PAPER CLIP AND BEND A DEEP HOOK AT ONE END.

4

BARE WIRE
COATING

BARE WIRE
COATING

WIND THE WIRE INTO A 2 ½-INCH CIRCULAR COIL WITH TWO LONG ENDS STICKING OUT AT OPPOSITE SIDES. WITH A DULL KNIFE, CAREFULLY SCRAPE AWAY THE INSULATING COATING ON THE UPPER SIDE OF EACH WIRE ONLY (SEE ALSO DIAGRAM IN PANEL OPPOSITE).

3

MAKE TWO SMALL HOLES AT THE SAME HEIGHT IN THE CENTER PANEL. PUSH THE PAPER CLIPS THROUGH. PLACE A DISK OR BUTTON MAGNET ON A PIECE OF THICK BOARD. POSITION IT ON THE BASE, HALFWAY BETWEEN THE PAPER CLIP HOOKS.

PUSH-AROUND

Electricity passing through the coil of wire makes it into an electromagnet. Its magnetic field pushes or pulls against the field of the permanent disk magnet, making the coil move and turn. But after a short distance the electricity stops since the wire coating now touches the paper clip and no electricity can pass. However, the coil's spinning motion carries it around farther until the bare wire again touches the paper clip, electricity flows, and...

ELECTRICITY THROUGH COIL PRODUCES MAGNETIC FIELD

PAPER CLIP TOUCHES BARE WIRE SO ELECTRICITY FLOWS

MAGNET REPELS COIL'S MAGNETIC FIELD AND PUSHES COIL AROUND FOR PART OF EACH TURN

MAGNET DOES NOT AFFECT WIRE

PAPER CLIP TOUCHES WIRE COATING SO NO ELECTRICITY FLOWS

COIL'S MOTION CARRIES IT AROUND THE REST OF EACH TURN

5

HANG THE WIRE COIL ON THE PAPER CLIP HOOKS. MAKE SURE THAT AS IT ROTATES IT COMES VERY NEAR THE MAGNET, BUT DOES NOT ACTUALLY TOUCH IT. ADD MORE LAYERS OF CARDBOARD UNDER THE MAGNET AS NECESSARY, TO ADJUST ITS HEIGHT.

MAKE CONNECTORS OUT OF ORDINARY WIRE AND PAPER CLIPS BETWEEN THE COIL AND BATTERY.

6

IN A SPIN

CONNECT THE BATTERY TO THE LARGE PAPER CLIPS. GIVE THE WIRE COIL A STARTING PUSH AND IT SHOULD SPIN ON ITS OWN. FOR THE BEST RESULTS YOU MAY HAVE TO ADJUST THE MAGNET'S POSITION AND RECHECK THE REMOVAL OF THE WIRE'S INSULATING COATING.

ELECTRIC SPLIT

Electricity flows very well through water. This is why it's so important never to touch electrical devices and appliances with wet hands or in damp conditions. Electricity also has an effect on water itself. It can make substances dissolved in the water move around—sometimes with very useful results.

Car wheels can be electroplated with the very hard, shiny metal called chromium. This chrome plating does not rust, and its shine lasts longer.

Solid silver items are very costly. Electro-plating silver onto cheaper metals makes them look expensive.

PROJECT: ELECTROPLATE A NAIL WITH COPPER

ELECTROPLATING

WARNING! Do this project in a well-ventilated area, as fumes are given off.

WHAT YOU NEED

- electrical wire
- paper clips
- large nail
- 9-volt battery
- vinegar
- cardboard
- glass jar
- glue
- bare copper wire
- tape
- salt

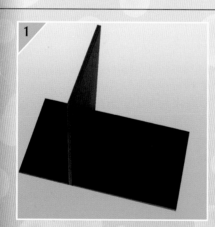

1. CUT A CARDBOARD BASE AND STAND 8 INCHES BY 5 INCHES. GLUE THE STAND ONTO THE BASE.

2. MAKE TWO CONNECTORS OF WIRE AND PAPER CLIPS TO LINK THE BATTERY TO THE ELECTRODES.

3. MAKE TWO HOLES IN THE UPPER STAND AND THREAD THROUGH THE WIRE CONNECTORS.

4. ATTACH THE CONNECTORS TO THE BATTERY BEHIND THE STAND.

5. PUSH THE NAIL AND PIECE OF COPPER WIRE THROUGH A STRIP OF CARDBOARD LONG ENOUGH TO FIT OVER THE GLASS OR JAR, AS SHOWN.

ELECTROLYSIS

Electricity passes through a liquid like water or vinegar between two contacts, or electrodes. When it does this, it can cause chemical reactions. This is called electrolysis. The electricity in the liquid makes positive ions at the copper electrode. These have a positive electric charge. The positive ions are attracted to the negative electrode, the nail.

POSITIVE BATTERY TERMINAL CONNECTED TO COPPER WIRE ELECTRODE

NEGATIVE BATTERY TERMINAL CONNECTED TO NAIL ELECTRODE

POSITIVE COPPER IONS STICK ONTO NEGATIVE NAIL

POUR THE VINEGAR INTO THE GLASS. ADD SOME SALT AND STIR WELL. PLACE THE CARDBOARD STRIP WITH THE NAIL AND COPPER WIRE OVER THE TOP. CONNECT THE BATTERY'S + TO THE COPPER AND THE − TO THE NAIL.

COPPER NAIL?
AFTER AN HOUR OR TWO, DISCONNECT THE BATTERY AND LIFT OUT THE NAIL. IT SHOULD BE COVERED WITH A GOLDEN-RED LAYER WHERE IT HAS BEEN IN THE VINEGAR. THIS IS COPPER PLATING MADE BY THE PROCESS OF ELECTROLYSIS.

LOOK AROUND

Using electricity to cover an item with a thin layer of another substance, usually a metal, is known as electroplating. It's a common way of protecting materials like steel that tend to tarnish, corrode, or rust.

HISTORY OF ELECTRICITY

600 B.C.E. Thales of ancient Greece saw that rubbing a piece of amber made it attract lightweight objects such as feathers. This was due to static electricity. But for centuries the attracting powers of electrical charges and magnetic fields were confused.

1600 William Gilbert's book suggested that the Earth is a huge magnet. He invented the name *electricity*.

1729 Stephen Gray discovered that electricity (as static charge) was on the outside of an object, not inside. He noted that electrical charges were carried or transmitted by certain substances but not others, discovering the idea of conductors and insulators.

1751 Benjamin Franklin described electricity as an invisible fluid and showed that it could make a needle into a magnet. The next year he carried out his dangerous kite experiment to show that lightning is a form of electrical discharge.

1773 Charles Dufay discovered that two rubbed pieces of amber repelled each other. He said that electricity was two sorts of fluid, depending on which substance was rubbed.

1786 Luigi Galvani noticed that a dead frog's legs twitched when touched with certain metals. He thought that "animal electricity" was made in living things.

1800 Alessandro Volta made a set of electrical cells, the "voltaic pile" - now called a battery.

1820 Hans Christian Oersted showed that a wire carrying electricity makes a magnetic field around it and affects a compass.

1820s Andre-Marie Ampère made many advances in electricity and electromagnetism, while William Sturgeon and Joseph Henry developed electromagnets.

1830s Michael Faraday devised early forms of electric generators and motors.

The first telegraphs used electricity to send long-distance messages.

1867 James Clerk Maxwell showed that electricity and magnetism were part of the same force, electromagnetism, and that light rays are waves of this force.

1904 John Ambrose Fleming invented the "vacuum tube" or valve, helping to start the science of electronics.

GLOSSARY

Ampere (amp) unit for measuring the amount of flow, or current, of electricity, or the number of electrons going past per second

Atom smallest piece or particle of a pure substance (chemical element). Two or more atoms joined together form a molecule.

Battery device that makes a flow of electricity from the chemicals inside. One "battery" on its own is really an electrical cell, while a true "battery" is many cells joined together.

Capacitor device for storing electrical charge, sometimes called a condenser (formerly a Leyden jar)

Charge An electron has a negative charge. The rest of the atom has a positive charge. Negative charge is shown by a minus sign (–) and positive charge is shown by a plus sign (+).

Conductor substance or material that carries electricity well

Current flow of electricity through a circuit of conductors

Electromagnet magnetic forces produced by the flow of electricity through a conductor (usually a coil of wire)

Electron particle that is part of an atom. It spins around the central part, or nucleus, of the atom.

Insulator substance or material that greatly resists the flow of electricity

Magnetic field area around a magnet where its magnetic force acts or is felt

Ohm unit for measuring the opposition or resistance of a substance to the flow of electricity

Pole in magnetism, one of two places in a magnet where the magnetic forces are strongest or most concentrated

Static electricity effects produced between electric charges which don't move

Volt unit for measuring the "pushing strength" of electricity, known as the potential difference (pd) or electromotive force (emf)

INDEX